CW00501630

Instant Vortex for Beginners

How to cook Fancy Meals with your Air Fryer for a Healthy Lifestyle

Taylor Rogers

Table of contents

BREAKFAST AND BRUNCH

1. Fried Potatoes

Servings: 4

Preparation Time: 5 minutes

Cooking Time: 25 minutes

Ingredients:

- Three large russet potatoes
- 1 tablespoon canola oil
- 1 tablespoon extra-virgin olive oil
- 1 teaspoon paprika
- One cup chopped onion
- One cup chopped red bell pepper
- One cup chopped green bell pepper
- Salt
- Pepper

Directions:

- Cut the potatoes into ½-inch cubes. Place the potatoes in a bowl of cold water and allow them to soak for at least thirty minutes, preferably an hour.
- Dry out the potatoes and wipe thoroughly with paper towels. Return them to the empty bowl.
- Add the canola and paprika, olive oils, and salt and pepper to flavor. Stir to fully coat the potatoes.
- Transfer the potatoes to the air fryer. Cook for twenty minutes, shaking the basket every five minutes (a total of four times).
- Put the onion and peppers to the basket. Fry for an additional three to four minutes.

Nutrition: Calories 279 Fat 8g Carbs 50g

2. Cherry Tarts

Servings: 6 Preparation Time: 15 minutes

Cooking Time: 20 minutes

Ingredients:

For the tarts:

- Two refrigerated piecrusts
- ⅓ Cup cherry preserves
- 1 teaspoon cornstarch
- Cooking oil

For the frosting:

- ½ cup vanilla yogurt 1-ounce cream cheese
- 1 teaspoon stevia Rainbow sprinkles

Directions:

- Place the piecrusts on a flat surface. Make use of a knife or pizza cutter, cut each piecrust into three rectangles, for six in total. (I discard the unused dough left from slicing the edges.)

- In a bowl, combine the preserves and cornstarch. Stir well.
- Scoop 1 tablespoon of the preserve mixture onto the top half of each piece of piecrust.
- Fold the bottom of each piece up to close the tart. Press along the edges of each tart to seal using the back of a fork.
- Sprinkle the breakfast tarts with cooking oil and place them in the oven. I do not recommend piling the breakfast tarts. They will stick together if piled. You may need to prepare them in two batches. Cook for ten minutesAllow the breakfast tarts to cool fully before removing from the air fryer.
- If needed, repeat steps 5 and 6 for the remaining breakfast tarts.

To make the frosting:

- In a bowl, mix the cream cheese, yogurt, and stevia. Mix well.

- Spread the breakfast tarts with frosting and top with sprinkles.

Nutrition: Calories 119 Fat 4g Carbs 19g

BREAD, PIZZA AND PASTA

3. Mozzarella Flatbread

Preparation Time: 5 minutes

Cooking Time: 5 minutes

Servings: 10

Ingredients:

- One tube prepared pizza dough
- 1/2 cup butter
- 1 teaspoon garlic
- Pinch of dried parsley
- Two cups mozzarella cheese, shredded

Directions:

- Open and unroll the pizza dough.
- From the long side, reroll the dough.
- Cut 1-inch rolls from dough and then flatten each roll.

- In a bowl, add the butter, garlic, and parsley and mix well.
- Brush the top of dough with butter mixture.
- Select the "Air Fry" mode.
- Press the Time button and set the cooking time to five minutes.
- Set the temperature at 350° F.
- Press Start button.
- When the unit beeps to show that it is preheated, open the lid.
- Arrange the rolls in greased "Air Fry Basket" and insert in the oven.
- Place the rolls onto a wire rack for about five minutes before serving.

Nutrition: Calories 126 Fat 12.1 g Carbs 2.8 g

4. New York Pizza

Preparation Time: 5 minutes

Cooking Time: 15 minutes

Servings: 4

Ingredients:

- One pizza dough
- One cup tomato sauce
- 14 ounces mozzarella cheese, freshly grated
- 2 ounces parmesan, freshly grated

Directions:

- Stretch your dough on a pizza peel lightly dusted with flour. Spread with a layer of tomato sauce.
- Top with mozzarella and parmesan cheese. Place on the baking tray.
- Bake in the preheated Air Fryer at 395° F for five minutes. Rotate the baking tray and bake for a further five minutes.

Nutrition: 308 Calories/ 4.1g Fat/ 25.7g Carbs

5. Nutty Bread Pudding

Preparation Time: 15 minutes

Cooking Time: 30 Minutes

Servings: 3

Ingredients:

- Eight slices of bread
- 1/2 cup buttermilk
- ¼ cup honey
- ¼ cup of sugar
- 4 tablespoon raisins
- One cup milk
- Two eggs
- 1/2 teaspoon vanilla extract
- 2 tablespoon butter, softened
- 2 tablespoon chopped hazelnuts
- Cinnamon for garnish

Directions:

- Preheat the Air fryer to 310 degrees F.

- Beat the eggs along with the honey, milk, buttermilk, vanilla, sugar, and butter.
- Mix in raisins and hazelnuts.
- Cut the bread into cubes and place them, in a bowl.
- Pour the milk mixture over the bread. Let soak for ten minutes. Cook the pudding for thirty minutes and garnish with cinnamon.

Nutrition: Calories 432 Fat 21g Total Carbs 54g

SNACKS AND APPETIZERS

6. Cheesy Dip

Preparation Time: 10 Minutes

Cooking Time: 30 minutes Servings: 12

Ingredients:

- 1/2 cup mayonnaise 1 small onion, diced
- 4 oz cream cheese, cubed
- 1 1/2 cups mozzarella cheese, shredded
- 1 1/2 cups cheddar cheese, shredded

Directions:

- Add all ingredients into the mixing bowl and mix until well combined.
- Pour mixture into the prepared baking dish.
- Set to bake at 400 degrees F for 35 minutes. After 5 minutes place the baking dish in the preheated oven.

Nutrition: Calories 140 Fat 11.9 g Carbs 3.4 g

7. Sweet Potato Fries

Preparation Time: 10 Minutes

Cooking Time: 16 minutes

Servings: 2

Ingredients:

2 sweet potatoes, peeled and cut into fries' shape

- 1 tablespoon olive oil
- Salt

Directions:

- Toss sweet potato fries with oil and salt and place in the air fryer basket then place the air fryer basket in the baking pan.
- Place a baking pan on the oven rack. Set to air fry at 375 degrees F for 16 minutes.

Nutrition: Calories 178 Fat 7.2 g Carbs 27.9 g

8. Zucchini Chips

Preparation Time: 10 minutes

Cooking time: 30 minutes

Servings: 6

Ingredients:

- Three zucchinis, thinly sliced
- Salt and black pepper to the taste
- 2 tbsp. olive oil
- 2 tbsp. balsamic vinegar

Directions:

- In a bowl, mix oil with vinegar, salt and pepper and whisk well.
- Add zucchini slices, toss to coat well, introduce in your air fryer and cook at 350 degrees F for 30 minutes.
- Divide zucchini chips into bowls and serve them cold as a snack.

Nutrition: Calories 100 Fat 3g Carbs 6g

9. Egg Roll Wrapped with Cabbage and Prawns

Preparation Time: 10 minutes

Cooking Time: 40 minutes

Servings: 4

Ingredients:

- 2 tbsp vegetable oil
- 1-inch piece fresh ginger, grated
- 1 tbsp minced garlic 1 egg
- 1 carrot, cut into strips
- 8 egg roll wrappers ¼ cup chicken broth
- 2 tbsp reduced-sodium soy sauce
- 1 cup shredded Napa cabbage
- 1 tbsp sesame oil 8 cooked prawns, minced
- 1 tbsp sugar

Directions:

- In a skillet over high heat, heat vegetable oil, and cook ginger and garlic for 40 seconds, until fragrant.

Stir in carrot and cook for another 2 minutes Pour in chicken broth, soy sauce, and sugar and bring to a boil.

- Add cabbage and let simmer until softened, for 4 minutes Remove skillet from the heat and stir in sesame oil. Let cool for 15 minutes Strain cabbage mixture, and fold in minced prawns. Whisk an egg in a small bowl. Fill each egg roll wrapper with prawn mixture, arranging the mixture just below the center of the wrapper.
- Fold the bottom part over the filling and tuck under. Fold in both sides and tightly roll up. Use the whisked egg to seal the wrapper. Repeat until all egg rolls are ready. Place the rolls into a greased air fryer basket, spray them with oil and cook for 12 minutes at 370 F, turning once halfway through.

Nutrition: Calories 215 Fat 7.9 g Carbs 6.7 g

MAINS

10. Honey Glazed Chicken Drumsticks

Preparation Time: 15 minutes

Cooking Time: 22 minutes

Servings: 4

Ingredients:

- ¼ cup Dijon mustard
- 1 tablespoon honey
- ½ tablespoon fresh rosemary, minced
- 1 tablespoon fresh thyme, minced
- 4 (6-ounces) boneless chicken drumsticks
- Salt and ground black pepper
- 2 tablespoons olive oil

Directions:

- In a bowl, mix well the mustard, honey, oil, herbs, salt, and black pepper. Add the drumsticks and generously coat with the mixture. Cover and refrigerate to marinate overnight.
- Set the temperature of Air Fryer to 320 degrees F. Grease an Air Fryer basket. Arrange the chicken drumsticks into the prepared Air Fryer basket in a single layer.
- Air Fry for about 12 minutes. Now, set the temperature of Air Fryer to 355 degrees F.
- Air Fry for 5-10 more minutes. Remove from Air Fryer and transfer the chicken drumsticks onto a serving platter.

Nutrition: Calories 377 Carbs 5.9g Protein 47.6g Fat 3.6g

11. Lemon Lentils and Fried Onion

Preparation time: 10 minutes

Cooking time: 30 minutes

Servings: 4

Ingredients:

- Four cups of water
- Cooking oil spray as needed
- One medium onion, peeled and cut into ¼ inch thick rings
- ½ cup kale stems removed
- Three large garlic cloves, pressed
- 2 tbsp. fresh lemon juice
- 2 tsp. nutritional yeast
- 1 tsp. salt
- 1 tsp. lemon zest
- ¾ tsp. fresh pepper

Directions:

- Preheat your Air Fryer to 392 degrees F

- Take a large-sized pot and bring lentils to boil over medium-high heat
- Adjust the heat into low and simmer for 30 minutes, making sure to stir after every 5 minutes
- Once they are cooked, take your Air Fryer basket and spray with cooking oil, add onion rings and sprinkle salt
- Fry for 5 minutes, shaking basket and fry for 5 minutes more
- Remove the basket and spray with oil. Cook for 5 minutes more until crispy and browned
- Add kale to the lentils and stir, add sliced greens
- Stir in garlic, lemon juice, yeast, salt, pepper, and stir well
- Top with crispy onion rings

Nutrition: Calories: 220 Fat: 1g Carbs: 39g Protein: 15g

12. Lemony Tuna

Preparation Time: 10 Minutes

Cooking Time: 10 Minutes

Servings: 4

Ingredients:

- 2 (6-ounce) cans water packed plain tuna
- 2 teaspoons Dijon mustard
- ½ cup breadcrumbs
- One egg
- Air fryer of hot sauce
- 1 tablespoon fresh lime juice
- 2 tablespoons fresh parsley, chopped
- 3 tablespoons canola oil
- Salt and freshly ground black pepper

Directions:

- Drain most of the liquid from the canned tuna. In a bowl, add the fish, mustard, crumbs, citrus juice, parsley and hot sauce and mix till well combined. Add a little canola oil if it seems too dry. Add egg, salt and stir to combine. Make the patties from tuna mixture. Refrigerate the tuna patties for about 2 hours.

- Pour into the Oven rack/basket. Place the Rack on the middle-shelf of the Smart Air Fryer Oven. Set temperature to 355°F, and set time to 12 minutes.

Nutrition: Calories 203 Fat 4.7g Protein 22g

POULTRY

13. Lemon Pepper Drumsticks

Preparation Time: 5 minutes

Cooking Time: 25 minutes

Servings: 8

Ingredients:

- 8 chicken drumsticks
- 4 tbsp. Salted butter; melted
- 2 tsp. Baking powder
- 1/2 tsp. Garlic powder
- 1 tbsp. lemon-pepper seasoning

Directions:

- Sprinkle the baking powder and the garlic powder over drumsticks and rub into the skin of the chicken-place the drumsticks in the basket of the air fryer.

- Adjust the temperature to 375°F and set the timer for twenty-five minutes
- Use tongs to turn drumsticks halfway through the cooking time. When the skin is golden brown, and the internal temperature is at least 165°F, remove from the air fryer.
- Take a large bowl, mix butter, and lemon pepper seasoning. Add drumsticks to the bowl and stir until coated.

Nutrition: Calories: 532 kcal/Cal Carbs: 1.2 g Protein: 48.3 g Fat: 32.3

14. Mustard Turkey Bites

Preparation Time: 5 minutes

Cooking Time: 20 minutes

Servings: 4

Ingredients:

- 1 big turkey breast, skinless; boneless, and cubed
- 4 garlic cloves; minced
- 1 tbsp. mustard
- 1 1/2 tbsp. extra-virgin olive oil
- Salt and pepper

Directions:

- Take a bowl and mix the chicken with the garlic and the other ingredients and toss.
- Put the turkey in the basket of your air fryer, cook at 360°F for twenty minutes, divide among plates and serve with a side salad.

Nutrition: Calories: 240 kcal/Cal Carbs: 6 g Fat: 12 g Protein: 15g

15. Nutmeg Chicken Thighs

Preparation Time: 15 minutes

Cooking Time: 20 minutes

Servings: 4

Ingredients:

- 2 lb. chicken thighs
- 1/2 tsp. nutmeg, ground
- A pinch of salt and pepper
- 2 tbsp. Olive oil

Directions:

- Season the chicken thighs with salt and pepper and rub with the rest of the ingredients.
- Place chicken thighs in the basket of the air fryer, cook at 360°F for fifteen minutes on each side, divide among plates.

Nutrition: Calories: 271 kcal/Cal Carbs: 6 g Fat: 12 g Protein: 13 g

16. Chicken Parmesan

Preparation Time: 5minutes

Cooking Time: 225 minutes

Serving: 2

Ingredients:

- 2 sizeable white meat chicken breasts, approximately 5-6 ounces
- One cup of breadcrumbs (Panko brand works well)
- 2 medium-sized eggs
- 1 tablespoon of dried oregano
- One cup of marinara sauce
- 2 slices of provolone cheese
- 1 tablespoon of parmesan
- Pinch of salt and pepper

Directions:

- Cover the air fryer's basket with a foil liner, leaving the edges uncovered to allow air to circulate through the basket.

- Preheat the air fryer to 350 degrees.
- In a bowl, beat the eggs until, the yolks and whites are fully combined, and set aside.
- In a separate bowl, combine the bread crumbs, salt, oregano and pepper, and set aside.
- One by one, dip the raw chicken breasts into the bowl with the dry ingredients, coating both sides, dipping into the bowl with wet ingredients, and then dropping back into the dry ingredients.
- Lay the coated chicken breasts on the foil covering the air fryer basket in a single flat layer.
- Set the air fryer timer for ten minutes.
- The air fryer will turn off, and the chicken should be halfway cooked and the breaded coating should begin to brown.
- Using tongs, turn each piece of chicken over to ensure complete frying.
- Set the air fryer to 320 degrees for another ten minutes.

- While the chicken is cooking, pour half the marinara sauce into a 7-inch heatproof skillet.
- After fifteen minutes, when the air fryer shuts off, remove the fried chicken breasts with tongs and set in the marinara-covered pan. Pour the rest of the marinara sauce over the fried chicken, then place the provolone slices on top both and spread the parmesan cheese all over the pan.
- Reset the air fryer to 350 degrees for 5 minutes.
- After 5 minutes, when the air fryer shuts off, remove the dish from the air fryer using tongs or oven mitts. The chicken will be perfectly crisped and the cheese melted and lightly toasted.

17. Fried Chicken Roast Served with Fruit Compote

Preparation Time: 15 minutes

Cooking Time: 50 minutes

Servings: 12

Ingredients:

- One full chicken, dissected 2 tablespoons olive oil
- 2 tablespoons chopped garlic
- 12 dried apricots, sliced 16 dried figs, coarsely chopped
- 1 tablespoon chopped fresh thyme
- 1 tablespoon chopped fresh rosemary
- Fruit Compote
- One apple, diced
- 1/2 cup red grapes, halved, seeds removed
- 1/2 cup chopped red onion
- 1/2 cup cider vinegar
- 1/2 cup dry white wine
- 2 teaspoons liquid stevia

- 2 1/2 teaspoon salt
- 1 1/2 teaspoon pepper

Directions:

- In a small bowl, mix together garlic, thyme, rosemary, salt, and pepper and rub the mixture over the pork.
- Light your air fryer and set it to 320°F, place the chicken on the basket and cook for ten minutes.
- Increase the temperature and cook for another ten minutes, turning the chicken pieces once. Increase the temperature once more time to 400° F and cook for five minutes to get a crispy finish.
- Make Fruit Compote: In a saucepan, combine all ingredients and cook over medium heat, stirring, for about twenty-five minutes.
- Once the chicken is cooked, serve hot with a spoon of fruit compote

Nutrition: Calories: 511 kcal, Carbs: 15 g, Fat: 36.8 g, Protein: 31.5 g

18. Roasted Chicken

Preparation Time: 10minutes

Cooking time: 25 minutes

Servings: 4

Ingredients:

- 6 lb. whole chicken
- 1 tbsp. minced garlic
- One white onion, peeled and halved
- 3 tbsp. butter
- 1 tsp. olive oil

Directions:

- Pre-heat the fryer at 360°F.
- Massage the chicken with oil and the minced garlic.
- Place the peeled and halved onion, as well as the butter, inside of the chicken.
- Cook the chicken in the fryer for 75 minutes.
- Take care when removing the chicken from the fryer, then carve.

19. Chicken Tenders

Preparation Time: 10 Minutes

Cooking Time: 12 minutes

Servings: 4

Ingredients:

- One lb chicken tenderloin
- Three eggs, lightly beaten
- 1/2 cup all-purpose flour
- 1/3 cup bread crumb
- Salt and Pepper
- Two tablespoon extra-virgin olive oil

Directions:

- Select air fry, set temperature 330 degrees F, timer for twelve minutes.
- In a shallow dish, stir flour, salt, and pepper. Add bread crumbs in a separate dish. Add one egg in a small bowl.
- Roll chicken in flour then dips in egg and coat with bread crumbs.

- Place coated chicken on roasting pan and cook.

Nutrition: Calories 296 Fat 11.5 g Carbs 18.7 g Protein 29.9 g

RED MEAT

20. Egg and Bell Pepper with Beef

Servings: 4

Preparation Time: 10 Minutes

Cooking Time: 30 minutes

Ingredients:

- 1-pound ground beef
- Six cups eggs, beaten
- One green bell pepper, seeded and chopped
- One onion, chopped
- Three cloves of garlic, minced
- 3 tablespoons olive oil

- Salt and pepper

Directions:

- Preheat the oven for five minutes with baking pan insert.
- In a baking dish stir the ground beef, olive oil, onion, garlic, and bell pepper. Dress with salt and pepper.
- Pour in the beaten eggs and give a good mix.
- Place the dish with the beef and egg mixture in the air fryer.
- Bake for thirty minutes at 330 degrees F.

Nutrition: Calories: 579; Carbs: 14.5g; Protein: 65.8g; Fat: 28.6g

21. Beef and Pasta Casserole

Preparation time: 10 minutes

Cooking time: 20 minutes

Servings: 4

Ingredients:

- One pound ground beef
- Seventeen ounces pasta
- One yellow onion, peeled and chopped
- One carrot, peeled and chopped
- One celery stalk, chopped
- Thirteen ounces mozzarella cheese, shredded
- Sixteen ounces tomato puree
- 1 tablespoon red wine
- 2 tablespoons butter
- Salt and ground pepper

Directions:

In a baking pan add the butter and melt. Add the onion carrot, and celery, stir and cook for five minutes. Include the meat, salt and pepper and cook for ten minutes. Add wine, stir and cook for one minute.

Add pasta, tomato puree and water to cover the pasta, stir, cover and cook for six minutes.

Add cheese, stir, divide among plates.

Nutrition: Calories: 182, Fat: 1g, Carbs: 31g, Protein: 12g

SEAFOOD

22. Salmon and Cauliflower Rice

Preparation Time: 30 minutes

Cooking Time: 40 minutes

Servings: 4

Ingredients:

- Four salmon fillets; boneless
- ½ cup chicken stock
- 1 cup cauliflower, riced
- 1 tsp. turmeric powder
- Salt and pepper
- 1 tbsp. butter; melted

Directions:

- In a pan that fits your air fryer, mixes the cauliflower rice with the other ingredients except the salmon, and toss

- Arrange the salmon fillets over the cauliflower rice, put the pan in the fryer, and bake at 360 degrees F for twenty-five minutes, flipping the fish after fifteen minutes

Nutrition: Calories: 241; Fat: 12g; Carbs: 6g; Protein: 12g

23. Salmon and Coconut Sauce

Preparation Time: 25 minutes

Cooking Time: 20 minutes

Servings: 4

Ingredients:

- 4 salmon fillets; boneless ½ cup coconut; shredded
- ¼ cup coconut cream
- 1/3 cup heavy cream
- ¼ cup lime juice
- 1 tsp. lime zest; grated
- A pinch of salt and pepper

Directions:

- Take a bowl and mix all the ingredients except the salmon and whisk.
- Arrange the fish in a pan that fits your air fryer, drizzle the coconut sauce all over, put the pan in the machine, and cook at 360 degrees F for twenty minutes

Nutrition: Calories: 227; Fat: 12g; Carbs: 4g; Protein: 9g

24. Salmon and Sauce

Preparation Time: 25 minutes

Cooking Time: 20 minutes

Servings: 4

Ingredients:

- 4 salmon fillets; boneless
- 2 garlic cloves; minced
- 1 tbsp. Chives; chopped.
- 1 tsp. lemon juice
- ¼ cup ghee; melted
- ½ cup heavy cream
- 1 tsp. Dill; chopped.
- A pinch of salt and black pepper

Directions:

- Take a bowl and mix all the ingredients except the salmon, and whisk well.

- Arrange the salmon in a pan that fits the air fryer, drizzle the sauce all over, introduce the pan in the machine, and cook at 360 degrees F for twenty minutes.

Nutrition: Calories: 220; Fat: 14g; Carbs: 5g; Protein: 12g

25. Salmon Dill Patties

Preparation Time: 10 minutes

Cooking Time: 15 minutes

Servings: 2

Ingredients:

- One egg
- tsp. dill weeds
- 1/2 cup almond flour
- 14 oz. salmon
- 1/4 cup onion, diced

Directions:

- Place the air fryer Basket onto the Baking Pan and spray air fryer basket with cooking spray.
- Add all ingredients into the bowl and stir well.
- Make patties from bowl mixture and place onto the air fryer basket.
- Set to air fry at 375 degrees F for ten minutes.

Nutrition: Calories 350 Fat 18 g Carbs 3 g Protein 44 g

VEGETABLES

26. Gold Ravioli

Preparation Time: 10minutes

Cooking Time: 6 minutes

Serving: 4

Ingredients:

- 1/2 cup panko bread crumbs
- Two teaspoons nutritional yeast
- One teaspoon dried basil
- One teaspoon dried oregano
- One teaspoon garlic powder
- Salt and ground black pepper
- ¼ cup aquafaba
- 8 ounces ravioli
- Cooking spray

Directions:

- Cover the fry basket with aluminum foil and coat with a light coat of oil.
- Preheat the fryer oven to 400°F. Combine panko bread crumbs, nutritional yeast, basil, oregano and garlic powder. Sprinkle with salt and pepper.
- Place the aquafaba in a separate bowl. Dip the ravioli in the aquafaba before tossing in the panko mixture. Spray with cooking spray and transfer to frying basket. Insert the frying basket in the center position.
- Select Air Fry and set the time to 6 minutes. Shake the fry basket halfway through

SOUPS

27. Italian Chicken Soup

Preparation Time: 35 minutes

Cooking Time: 30 minutes

Servings: 4

Ingredients:

- Three chicken breasts, one carrot, chopped
- One small zucchini, peeled and chopped
- One celery stalk, chopped
- One small onion, chopped
- One bay leaf
- 5 cups water; 6-7 black olives, pitted and halved
- ½ teaspoon. Salt; 1 teaspoon. Dried basil
- black pepper, fresh parsley, lemon juice, to serve

Directions:

- Place chicken breasts, onion, carrot, celery, and bay leaf in a deep soup pot. Add in salt, black pepper, basil, and water.
- Stir well and bring to a boil. Add zucchini and olives and reduce heat.
- Simmer for 30 minutes. Remove chicken from the pot and set aside to cool. Serve with lemon juice and sprinkled with parsley.

DESSERTS

Banana-Choco Brownies

Preparation Time: 5 minutes

Cooking Time: 30 minutes

Serving: 12

Ingredients:

- 2 cups almond flour
- 2 teaspoons baking powder
- ½ teaspoon baking powder
- ½ teaspoon baking soda
- ½ teaspoon salt
- 1 over-ripe banana
- 3 large eggs
- ½ teaspoon stevia powder
- ¼ cup of coconut oil
- 1 tablespoon vinegar

- 1/3 cup almond flour
- 1/3 cup cocoa powder

Directions:

- Preheat the air fryer oven for 5 minutes.
- Combine all ingredients in a food processor and pulse until well-combined.
- Pour into a baking dish that will fit in the air fryer.
- Place in the air fryer basket and cook for 30 minutes at 350°F or if a toothpick inserted in the middle comes out clean.

Nutrition: Calories: 75; Fat: 6.5g; Protein: 1.7g; Sugar: 2g

28. Chocolate Donuts

Preparation Time: 5 minutes

Cooking Time: 20 minutes

Serving: 8-10

Ingredients:

- (8-ounce) can jumbo biscuits
- Cooking oil
- Chocolate sauce, such as Hershey's

Directions:

- Separate the biscuit dough into eight biscuits and place them on a flat work surface. Use a small circle cookie cutter or a biscuit cutter to cut a hole in each biscuit center. You can also cut the holes using a knife.
- Spray the air fryer basket with cooking oil.
- Place four donuts in the oven. Do not stack. Spray with cooking oil. Set temperature to 350°F. Cook for 4 minutes.

- Open the air fryer and flip the donuts—Cook for an additional 4 minutes.
- Remove the cooked donuts from the oven, and then repeat for the remaining four donuts.
- Drizzle chocolate sauce over the donuts and enjoy while warm.

Nutrition: Calories: 181; Fat: 98g; Protein: 3g; Fiber: 1g

FRUITS

29. Vegan Tangerine Cake

Preparation time: 10 minutes

Cooking time: 20 minutes

Servings: 8

Ingredients:

- ¾ cup of coconut sugar
- 2 cups whole wheat flour
- ¼ cup olive oil
- ½ cup almond milk
- One tsp. cider vinegar
- ½ tsp. vanilla extract
- Juice and zest of 2 lemons
- Juice and zest of 1 tangerine

Directions:

- In a prepared bowl, mix flour with sugar and stir.
- In another bowl, mix oil with milk, lemon juice and zest, tangerine zest, flour, vinegar, vanilla extract, and whisk very well, pour this into a cake pan, introduce in the fryer and cook at 360 degrees F for 20 minutes.

Nutrition: Calories 210 Fat 1g Carbs 6g Protein 4g

DIABETIC RECIPES

30. Breakfast Bombs

(Prep Time: 10 minutes| Cook Time: 15 minutes| Servings: 3)

Ingredients

- Three eggs (large), lightly whisked
- Less-fat cream cheese: two tbsp. Softened
- Chopped chives: 1 tablespoon fresh
- Freshly prepared whole-wheat pizza dough: 1/4 cup or 4 ounces
- Cooking spray
- 3 pieces of bacon: center cut
- Freshly prepared whole-wheat pizza dough: 1/4 cup or 4 ounces Cooking spray

Instructions

- In a skillet, cook the bacon slices for about ten minutes. Crumble the cooked bacon. Add the eggs to the skillet and cook until loose for almost one minute. In another bowl, mix with chives, cheese, and bacon.
- Cut the dough into four pieces. Make it into a five-inch circle.
- Add 1/4 of egg mixture in the center of dough circle pieces.
- Seal the dough seams with water and pinch
- Add dough pockets in one single layer in the air fryer. Spray with cooking oil
- Cook for 5-6 minutes, at 350°F or until light golden brown.

Nutritional value: per serving: Calories 305| Fat 15g| Protein 19g| Carbohydrate 26g|Fiber 2g

31. Air Fryer Breakfast Toad-in-the-Hole Tarts

(Prep Time: 5 minutes| Cook Time: 25 minutes| Servings: 4)

Ingredients

- Chopped fresh chives: one tbsp.
- Frozen puff pastry: one sheet, thawed
- Eggs: four large
- Chopped ham: 4 tbsp. (cooked)
- Shredded: 4 tbsp. of Cheddar cheese

Instructions

- Let the air fryer preheat to 400 F
- Lay puff pastry on a clean surface and slice into four squares.
- Add two squares of puff pastry in the air fryer and cook for 8 minutes.
- Take out from the air fryer and make an indentation in the dough's center and add one tbsp. Of ham and one

tbsp. Of cheddar cheese in every hole. Add one egg to it.

- Return the basket to the air fryer.
- Let it cook to your desired doneness, for about six minutes or more.
- Take out from the basket of the air fryer.
- Cool for 5 minutes.
- Top with chives and serve hot

Nutritional value: Cal 154|fat 7g| carbs 7g|protein 10.1 g

32. Air Fried Cheesy Chicken Omelet

(Prep Time: 5 minutes| Cook Time: 18 minutes| Servings: 2)

Ingredients

- Cooked Chicken Breast: half cup (diced) divided
- Four eggs
- Onion powder: 1/4 tsp, divided
- Salt: 1/2 tsp., divided
- Pepper: 1/4 tsp., divided
- Shredded cheese: 2 tbsp. divided
- Garlic powder: 1/4 tsp, divided

Instructions

- Take two ramekins, grease with olive oil.
- Add two eggs to each ramekin. Add cheese with seasoning.
- Blend to combine. Add 1/4 cup of cooked chicken on top.

- Cook for 14-18 minutes, in the air fryer at 330 F, or until fully cooked.

Nutritional value: per serving: Calories 185 |Proteins 20g |Carbs 10g |Fat 5g |

Diabetic Turkey Recipes

33. Turkey Breast with Mustard Maple Glaze

(Prep Time: 10 minutes| Cook Time:55 minutes| Servings: 6)

Ingredients

- Whole turkey breast: 5 pounds
- Olive oil: 2 tsp.Maple syrup: 1/4 cup
- Dried sage: half tsp.
- Smoked paprika: half tsp.
- Dried thyme: one tsp.Salt: one tsp.
- Freshly ground black pepper: half tsp.
- Dijon mustard: 2 tbsp.

Instructions

- Let the air fryer preheat to 350 F

- Rub the olive oil all over the turkey breast
- In a bowl, mix salt, sage, pepper, thyme, and paprika. Mix well and coat turkey in this spice rub.
- Place the turkey in an air fryer, cook for 25 minutes at 350°F. Flip the turkey over and cook for another 12 minutes. Flip again and cook for another ten minutes. With an instant-read thermometer, the internal temperature should reach 165°F.
- In the meantime, in a saucepan, mix mustard, maple syrup, and with one tsp. of butter.
- Brush this glaze all over the turkey when cooked.
- Cook again for five minutes. Slice and Serve with fresh salad.

Nutritional value: per serving: Cal 379 | Fat: 23 g| Carbs: 21g | Protein: 52g

Diabetic Fish & Seafood Recipes

34. Air Fried Cajun Salmon

(Prep Time: 10 minutes| Cook Time:20 minutes| Servings: 1)

Ingredients

- Fresh salmon: 1 piece
- Cajun seasoning: 2 tbsp.
- Lemon juice.

Instructions

- Let the air fryer preheat to 180 C.
- Pat dry the salmon fillet. Rub lemon juice and Cajun seasoning over the fish fillet.
- Place in the air fryer, cook for 7 minutes. Serve with salad greens and lime wedges.

Nutritional value: per serving: 216 Cal| total fat 19g |carbohydrates 5.6g |protein 19.2g

35. Air Fryer Shrimp Scampi

(Prep Time: 5 minutes| Cook Time:10 minutes| Servings: 2)

Ingredients

- Raw Shrimp: 4 cups
- Lemon Juice: 1 tablespoon
- Chopped fresh basil
- Red Pepper Flakes: 2 teaspoons
- Butter: 2.5 tablespoons
- Chopped chives
- Chicken Stock: 2 tablespoons
- Minced Garlic: 1 tablespoon

Instructions

- Let the air fryer preheat with a metal pan to 330F
- In the hot pan, add garlic, red pepper flakes, and half of the butter. Let it cook for two minutes.
- Add the butter, shrimp, chicken stock, minced garlic, chives, lemon juice, basil to the pan. Let it cook for five minutes. Bathe the shrimp in melted butter.

- Take out from the air fryer and let it rest for one minute.
- Add fresh basil leaves and chives and serve.

Nutritional value: per serving: 287 Kcal |total fat 5.5g |carbohydrates 7.5g | protein 18g

Diabetic Pork Recipes

36. Air Fryer Tasty Egg Rolls

(Prep Time: 10 minutes| Cook Time:20 minutes| Servings: 3)

Ingredients

- Coleslaw mix: half bag
- Half onion
- Salt: 1/2 teaspoon
- Half cups of mushrooms
- Lean ground pork: 2 cups
- One stalk of celery
- Wrappers (egg roll)

Instructions

- Put a skillet over medium flame, add onion and lean ground pork and cook for 5-7 minutes.

- Add coleslaw mixture, salt, mushrooms, and celery to skillet and cook for almost five minutes.
- Lay egg roll wrapper flat and add filling (1/3 cup), roll it up, seal with water.
- Spray with oil the rolls.
- Put in the air fryer for 6-8 minutes at 400F, flipping once halfway through.
- Serve hot.

Nutritional value: per serving: Cal 245| Fat: 10g| Net Carbs: 9g|Protein: 11g

Diabetic Beef Recipes

37. Air Fryer Beef Steak Kabobs with Vegetables

(Prep Time: 30 minutes| Cook Time:10 minutes| Servings: 4)

Ingredients

- Light Soy sauce: 2 tbsp.
- Lean beef chuck ribs: 4 cups, cut into one-inch pieces
- Low-fat sour cream: 1/3 cup
- Half onion
- 8 skewers: 6 inch
- One bell peppers

Instructions

- In a mixing bowl, add soy sauce and sour cream, mix well. Add the lean beef chunks, coat well, and let it marinate for half an hour or more.

- Cut onion, bell pepper into one-inch pieces. In water, soak skewers for ten minutes.
- Add onions, bell peppers, and beef on skewers; alternatively, sprinkle with Black Pepper
- Let it cook for 10 minutes in a preheated air fryer at 400F, flip halfway through.
- Serve with yogurt dipping sauce.

Nutritional Value: per serving: Calories 268 |Proteins 20g |Carbs 15g|Fat 10g |

Diabetic Chicken Recipes

38. Lemon-Garlic Chicken

(Prep Time: 2 hours' minutes| Cook Time: 35 minutes| Servings: 4)

Ingredients

- Lemon juice ¼ cup
- 1 Tbsp. olive oil
- 1 tsp mustard
- Cloves of garlic
- ¼ tsp salt
- ⅛ tsp black pepper
- Chicken thighs
- Lemon wedges

Instructions

- In a bowl, whisk together the olive oil, lemon juice, mustard Dijon, garlic, salt, and pepper.
- Place the chicken thighs in a large ziploc bag. Spill marinade over chicken & seal bag, ensuring all chicken parts are covered. Cool for at least 2 hours.
- Preheat a frying pan to 360 F (175 C).
- Remove the chicken with towels from the marinade, & pat dry.
- Place pieces of chicken in the air fryer basket, if necessary, cook them in batches.
- Fry till chicken is no longer pink on the bone & the juices run smoothly, 22 to 24 min. Upon serving, press a lemon slice across each piece.

Nutritional value: per serving: Cal 258|Fat: 18.6g| Carbs: 3.6g| Protein: 19.4g

39. Buttermilk Chicken in Air-Fryer

(Prep Time: 30 minutes| Cook Time:20 minutes| Servings: 6)

Ingredients

- Chicken thighs: 4 cups skin-on, bone-in

Marinade

- Buttermilk: 2 cups
- Black pepper: 2 tsp.
- Cayenne pepper: 1 tsp.
- Salt: 2 tsp.

Seasoned Flour

- Baking powder: 1 tbsp.
- All-purpose flour: 2 cups
- Paprika powder: 1 tbsp.
- Salt: 1 tsp.Garlic powder: 1 tbsp.

Instructions

- Let the air fry heat at 180 C.

- With a paper towel, pat dry the chicken thighs.
- In a mixing bowl, add paprika, black pepper, salt mix well, then add chicken pieces. Add buttermilk and coat the chicken well. Let it marinate for at least 6 hours.
- In another bowl, add baking powder, salt, flour, pepper, and paprika. Put one by one of the chicken pieces and coat in the seasoning mix.
- Spray oil on chicken pieces and place breaded chicken skin side up in air fryer basket in one layer, cook for 8 minutes, then flip the chicken pieces' cook for another ten minutes
- Take out from the air fryer and serve right away.

Nutritional value: per serving: Cal 210|fat 18 g| protein 22g|carbs 12 g

Diabetic Desserts Recipes

40. Air Fryer Thumbprint Cookies

(Prep Time: 15 minutes| Cook 10 minutes| Servings: 10)

Ingredients

- One teaspoon of baking powder One cup of almond flour
- Three tablespoons of natural low-calorie sweetener
- One large eggThree and a half tablespoons raspberry (reduced-sugar) preserves
- Four tablespoons of softened cream cheese

Instructions

- In a large bowl, add egg, baking powder, flour, sweetener, and cream cheese, mix well until a dough (wet) forms.
- Chill the dough in the fridge for almost 20 minutes, until dough is cool enough

- And then form into balls.
- Let the air fryer preheat to 400 F, add the parchment paper to the air fryer basket.
- Make ten balls from the dough and put them in the prepared air fryer basket.
- With your clean hands, make an indentation from your thumb in the center of every cookie. Add one teaspoon of the raspberry preserve in the thumb hole.
- Bake in the air fryer for seven minutes, or until light golden brown to your liking.
- Let the cookies cool completely in the parchment paper for almost 15 minutes, or they will fall apart.
- Serve with tea and enjoy.

Nutritional value: Per Serving: 111.6 calories| protein 3.7g| carbohydrates 9.1g| fat 8.6g

30-Day Meal Plan

This meal is designed to help you achieve the best health possible. Hope you enjoy these delicious recipes that will keep your belly full and glucose level under control for days to come.

Week 1

Monday (Day 1)

Breakfast: Bell Peppers Frittata

Lunch: Lemon Rosemary Chicken

Snack: Air-Fryer Kale Chips with dipping

Dinner: Air Fryer Pork Taquitos

Tuesday (Day 2)

Breakfast: Air Fryer Crisp Egg Cups

Lunch: Air-Fried Rosemary Garlic Grilled Prawns

Snack: Air Fryer Buffalo Cauliflower with dipping

Dinner: Air Fried Empanadas

Wednesday (Day 3)

Breakfast: Asparagus Frittata

Lunch: Crispy Air Fryer Fish

Snack: Air Fryer Onion Rings with dipping

Dinner: Air Fryer Lemon Garlic Shrimp

Thursday (Day 4)

Breakfast: Mushroom Oatmeal

Lunch: Chicken Fajitas

Snack: Air Fryer Chicken Nuggets

Dinner: Sriracha & Honey Tossed Calamari

Friday (Day 5)

Breakfast: Air Fryer Egg Rolls

Lunch: Air Fryer Delicata Squash

Snack: Zucchini Parmesan Chips

Dinner: Air Fryer Crispy Fish Sandwich

Saturday (Day 6)

Breakfast: Air Fryer Salmon cakes

Lunch: Air Fryer Popcorn Chicken

Snack: Zucchini Gratin

Dinner: Air Fryer Lemon Pepper Shrimp

Sunday (Day 7)

Breakfast: Air Fryer Egg Rolls

Lunch: Air Fryer Crispy Fish Sticks

Snack: One Blueberry Muffin

Dinner: Air-Fried Buttermilk Chicken

Week 2

Monday (Day 8)

Breakfast: Air-Fried Spinach Frittata

Lunch: Crispy Air Fryer Brussels Sprouts

Snack: Slice of Vegan Cake

Dinner: Air Fryer Turkey Breast

Tuesday (Day 9)

Breakfast: Mushroom Omelet

Lunch: Coconut Shrimp

Dinner: Juicy Turkey Burgers with Zucchini

Wednesday (Day 10)

Breakfast: Mushroom Oatmeal

Lunch: Air Fryer Fish and Chips

Snack: Slice of Berry Cheesecake

Dinner: Air Fryer Meatloaf

Thursday (Day 11)

Breakfast: Lemon-Garlic Tofu

Lunch: Air Fryer Hamburger

Snack: Slice of Carrot Cake

Dinner: Air-Fried Buttermilk Chicken

Friday (Day 12)

Breakfast: Air-fryer omelet

Lunch: Air Fried Empanadas

Snack: Zucchini Chips

Dinner: Air Fry Rib-Eye Steak

Saturday (Day 13)

Breakfast: Breakfast Bombs

Lunch: Orange Chicken Wings

Snack: Low Carb Pork Dumplings with Dipping Sauce

Dinner: Air Fryer Chicken & Broccoli

Sunday (Day 14)

Breakfast: Air-fryer baked eggs

Lunch: Air Fryer Low Carb Chicken Bites

Snack: Half Sugar Free Brownie

Dinner: Air-Fried Turkey Breast with Maple Mustard Glaze

Week 3

Monday (Day 15)

Breakfast: Crisp egg cups

Lunch: Sweet potato fries

Snack: One Apple Cider Donut

Dinner: Air Fryer Whole Wheat Crusted Pork Chops

Tuesday (Day 16)

Breakfast: Vegan Breakfast Sandwich

Lunch: Air Fryer Delicata Squash

Snack: Air Fryer Kale Chips

Dinner: Air-Fried Chicken Pie

Wednesday (Day 17)

Breakfast: Vegan mashed potato bowl

Lunch: Chicken Fajitas

Snack: One blueberry muffin

Dinner: Garlic Parmesan Crusted Salmon

Thursday (Day 18)

Breakfast: Toad in the hole tarts

Lunch: Air Fryer Low Carb Chicken Bites

Snack: Avocado fries

Dinner: Air Fryer Hamburger

Friday (Day 19)

Breakfast: Breakfast bombs

Lunch: Air Fryer Chicken & Broccoli

Snack: Onion rings

Dinner: Air Fryer Sesame Seeds Fish Fillet

Saturday (Day 20)

Breakfast: Mushroom Omelet

Lunch: Garlic Parmesan Crusted Salmon

Snack: Roasted corn

Dinner: Chicken Fajitas

Sunday (Day 21)

Breakfast: Avocado Egg Rolls

Lunch: Air Fryer Lemon Pepper Shrimp

Snack: Zucchini Parmesan Chips

Dinner: Air Fry Rib-Eye Steak

Week 4

Monday (Day 22)

Breakfast: Apple fritter

Lunch: Air-Fried Rosemary Garlic Grilled Prawns

Dinner: Mustard Glazed Air Fryer Pork Tenderloin

Tuesday (Day 23)

Breakfast: Lemon-Garlic Tofu

Lunch: Air Fryer Turkey Breast Tenderloin

Snack: Small slice of sugar-free berry cheesecake

Dinner: Air Fryer Lemon Pepper Shrimp

Wednesday (Day 24)

Breakfast: Vegan Breakfast Sandwich

Lunch: Air Fryer Chicken & Broccoli

Snack: Slice of Carrot Cake

Dinner: Air-Fried Rosemary Garlic Grilled Prawns

Thursday (Day 25)

Breakfast: Egg Air-Fryer Omelet

Lunch: Air Fryer Southwest Chicken

Snack: Air-fry Brownie

Dinner: Air Fryer Sesame Seeds Fish Fillet

Friday (Day 26)

Breakfast: Slice of eggless and vegan cake

Lunch: Air Fryer Low Carb Chicken Bites

Snack: Kale chips

Dinner: Air Fryer Turkey Breast Tenderloin

Saturday (Day 27)

Breakfast: Bell Pepper Frittata

Lunch: Air-Fried Buttermilk Chicken

Snack: Chicken Nuggets

Dinner: Air Fry Rib-Eye Steak

Sunday (Day 28)

Breakfast: Air-fryer Spanakopita Bites

Lunch: Orange Chicken Wings

Snack: One peanut butter cookie

Dinner: Air Fryer Hamburger

Week 5

Monday (Day 29)

Breakfast: Toad in the hole Tart

Lunch: Crab cakes

Snack: Air Fryer Roasted Corn

Dinner: Air Fried Empanadas

Tuesday (Day 30)

Breakfast: Banana muffin with coffee

Lunch: Lemon Rosemary Chicken

Snack: Egg rolls

Dinner: Air Fryer Delicata Squash

CPSIA information can be obtained
at www.ICGtesting.com
Printed in the USA
LVHW061634210621
690769LV00002B/30

9 781914 387296